Poems of Love, Life & Relationships

Poems of Love, Life & Relationships

Volume One

RICHARD BAYER

POEMS OF LOVE, LIFE & RELATIONSHIPS VOLUME ONE

Copyright © 2017 RICHARD BAYER.

All rights reserved. No part of this book may be used or reproduced by any means, graphic, electronic, or mechanical, including photocopying, recording, taping or by any information storage retrieval system without the written permission of the author except in the case of brief quotations embodied in critical articles and reviews.

iUniverse books may be ordered through booksellers or by contacting:

iUniverse
1663 Liberty Drive
Bloomington, IN 47403
www.iuniverse.com
1-800-Authors (1-800-288-4677)

Because of the dynamic nature of the Internet, any web addresses or links contained in this book may have changed since publication and may no longer be valid. The views expressed in this work are solely those of the author and do not necessarily reflect the views of the publisher, and the publisher hereby disclaims any responsibility for them.

Any people depicted in stock imagery provided by Thinkstock are models, and such images are being used for illustrative purposes only. Certain stock imagery © Thinkstock.

ISBN: 978-1-5320-3049-9 (sc)
ISBN: 978-1-5320-3048-2 (e)

Library of Congress Control Number: 2017912576

Print information available on the last page.

iUniverse rev. date: 10/18/2017

DEDICATION

I am dedicating this book to my wonderful wife, my fabulous children and all those other wonderful family members and friends who supported this effort, encouraging and propelling me into completing this work.

They have all made this adventure for me a memory I will cherish for the rest of my life.

Thank you all from the bottom of my heart! I love you!

SEE AND BE
By RICHARD BAYER

FOREGONE CONCLUSIONS
IN PROTECTIVE
ILLUSIONS
WILL LIMIT
THE VIEW
OF WHAT'S REALLY
TRUE;

BUT THE FEW
WHO BELIEVE
IN WHAT THEY
CONCEIVE
CAN BE
WHATEVER
THEY SEE!

AUTHOR'S NOTE

I wrote the poems included in this book over many years and decided recently to publish them. During those years I shared these poems with only a handful of friends and family members as I wrote them primarily to set my thoughts to paper.

As a result of the urgings of some folks close to me, I decided to edit and organize these poems to ready them for publication. Being aware of the fact that poetry is, commercially, the least popular form of literature and that I am an unknown first-time writer, I have no illusions of becoming immensely famous or hugely successful in this endeavor. I am, however, enjoying the process of self-publishing despite having to endure long hours and frustrations with software and my computer probably due mostly to my age and inexperience with both.

The incredibly generous support I've received throughout this adventure from dedicated family and friends kept me going and helped me arrive to this point. In addition, I am very grateful to a number of people, including Alexis Folz, my fabulous pre-viewer, who helped select which of my poem samples to send to my subscribers on a weekly basis until publication and Sarah Laufer. Sarah is a volunteer at the Memorial Sloan Kettering Cancer Center's "Visible Ink Writing Program," for patients of the hospital, who gave so generously of her time in reviewing and editing my work and arranging the order of the poems, all of which helped tremendously in getting me through the writing and publishing process. Both of these young ladies were absolutely delightful to work with. I'm also very grateful to Judith Kelman, Director of the "Visible Ink Writing Program" for selecting Sarah to work with me. In addition, I am indebted to the folks at iUNIVERSE, especially Amanda Webb for her endless patience in sweetly and politely answering my innumerable questions day after day to Andrea Adonis, Casey Martin and Earl Thomas for kindly and professionally leading me through the self-publishing process of this book.

To all my readers:
I'd love to hear from you. Please write to me at RBAYER@RBAYERPOEMS.COM.

Richard Bayer, September, 2017

Contents

POEMS I
LOVE LOST

WITH INFINITE GRACE	3
LOVE DIES	4
WITHOUT YOU	6
THE TRAP	7
THE COMMON LIE	8
THE PEOPLE PROBLEM	9
MY FLAME ETERNAL	10
NOT YET	11
I SEE YOUR FACE	12
NOW AND THEN	13
ALONE IN MY OFFICE	14
YESTERDAY I SAW THE RIVER	16
THE MATTER OF AGE	17
THE DAY IN THE PARK	19
SILENT PARTNER	23
RETURN TO MARYLAND	25
STANDING TREE	27
YOUR SILENCE CALLS	29
ALWAYS NOW	31
THE KINGDOM	33

POEMS II
SEEKING LOVE...AGAIN

I AWAIT YOUR COMING	37
IF I COULD	39
NO LIES	40

REALLY THERE	41
SELF DEFEAT	43
VERIFICATION	44
GOT TO SEE YOU AGAIN	45
THE SECRET IN YOUR EYES	46
YOU AND I	48
WHAT MIGHT HAVE BEEN	50
IN QUIET DESPERATION	51
HAVING NOT YOUR LOVE	53
ENCOUNTER	55
DON'T LAUGH AT ME	57
DID YOU EVER NOTICE…?	59
CONFLICT	60
BEWARE	61
A PLEA	62
AFTERTHOUGHT	63
ON RARE OCCASION	64
A DECISION	65
CHANGING MOOD	67

POEMS III
LOVE FOUND

WHAT A WAY TO START THE DAY	71
YOUR KISS	73
HEART TO HEART	75
YOUR VOICE WITHIN THE BREEZE	77
GLAD	78
FALLING IN LOVE	80
MY LOVE FOR YOU WILL BE	82
THE FEAR OF LOSING YOU	84
LIKE TIME ALONE	85

NO DOUBT ABOUT IT	87
WALK WITH ME	88
A PROMISE TRUE	93

POEMS IV
FOR THOSE I LOVE
FOR MY WIFE

FOR ETERNITY	96
A LITTLE RUBBER DUCK	97
FOR MY WIFE ON HER BIRTHDAY	99
ON OUR FIRST ANNIVERSARY	101
I WOULD MARRY YOU AGAIN	103
SHORTNESS IS THE KEY	105
WHEN THE SONG IS OVER	110

POEMS V
FOR THOSE I LOVE
FOR SPECIAL PEOPLE / SPECIAL OCCASIONS

LITTLE GIRL WITH THE WHITE COAT ON	115
MY 25TH HIGH SCHOOL REUNION	116
MY BABY	121
MY FABULOUS PRE-VIEWER	126
THE FIRST TIME YOU SAID "HI DAD"	127
CHRISTMAS IS MY FAVORITE TIME OF YEAR	129
CHRISTMAS LULLABY	131
CHRISTMAS TIME IS CHILDREN'S TIME	132
THE ALPHABET SONG	134
"WHAT DID YOU SAY?"	136

POEMS VI
INTROSPECTING

SEE AND BE	141
ALL OR NOTHING	142
ALMOSTS	143

AMERICA'S BEST	144
EACH OF US	146
I SEE YOU DEATH	150
IN ABSOLUTE DEVOTION	152
IT'S TIME	153
LIFE WON'T STAND STILL	154
LOVE IS LIKE A CHILD	156
LOVE POEMS	158
LOVE	159
NO CONTEST	160
OPPORTUNITY	161
PASSING FORTY	162
RUNNIN'	165
THE KEY	167
THE PREDATOR	168
THE TRUTH	169
TWO ALTERNATIVES	170
UNREQUITED LOVE	171
WAR	172
YOU CAN'T GIVE LOVE TO ANYONE	173
YOUR CHOICE	174

POEMS OF LOVE, LIFE & RELATIONSHIPS

POEMS I

LOVE LOST

POEMS OF LOVE, LIFE & RELATIONSHIPS

POEMS

LOVE LOST

WITH INFINITE GRACE

WITH INFINITE GRACE,

TOO RAPID A PACE,

SHE DANCED

THROUGH MY LIFE,

TOUCHING MY HEART,

TORN NOW APART,

NEVER

TO BE WHOLE

AGAIN!

LOVE DIES

LOVE DIES

AND REAPPEARS

BEFORE MY EYES

WITH CRIES

OF GRIEF

AND DISBELIEF;

NO RELIEF

WILL IT AFFORD –

AT LEAST

   NOT BY

   ITS OWN ACCORD;

NOT EVEN

THE SWORD

    OF YOUR GOODBYE

WILL SEVER

    ITS TIE...

AND LET IT DIE...

    FOREVER!

WITHOUT YOU

LIFE,

FATALLY UNBORN...

BEAUTY,

HIDEOUSLY VEILED...

LOVE,

WASTEFULLY UNSPENT...

WITHOUT YOU!

THE TRAP

THERE'S AN ELEMENT

OF TRUTH

IN EVERY SINGLE LIE;

THAT'S WHAT MAKES THEM

EASY TO BELIEVE...

LIKE

THE LAST TIME

YOU TOLD ME...

"I LOVE YOU"!

THE COMMON LIE

YOU LIED!

YOU SAID

YOU WANTED THE TRUTH...

AND I GAVE IT TO YOU!

I KNOW YOU LIED

BECAUSE I HAVEN'T HEARD

FROM YOU

SINCE!

THE PEOPLE PROBLEM

IN REVEALING
MY TRUE FEELINGS,
I HAVE FOUND
MYSELF
COMING BACK

AGAIN AND AGAIN
TO THE SAME
TIRESOME CONCLUSION:

IN THE RAREST INSTANCES,
I TRUSTED YOU;

IN THE MOST COMMON,
I DIDN'T;

AND

IN THE FRUSTRATING MIDDLE,
I AM ANGRY
WITH MYSELF
FOR MAKING THE MISTAKE
OF HAVING EVER TRUSTED
YOU...

AT ALL.

MY FLAME ETERNAL

MY FLAME ETERNAL

WARMS

THE NIGHT

AND

LIGHTS

THE DAY,

ANXIOUSLY

AWAITING

YOUR

RETURN.

NOT YET

IN REPRESSING

MY OBSESSION,

I'M DEPRESSING

MY EXPRESSION;

I SHOULD

LET GO...

AND LET IT

SHOW;

BUT, I CAN'T –

NOT YET –

NOT YET!

I SEE YOUR FACE

I SEE YOUR FACE
    IN EVERYTHING
        THAT'S BEAUTIFUL;

I FEEL YOUR TOUCH
    IN EVERYTHING
        THAT'S SOFT;

I TASTE YOUR LIPS
    IN EVERY SIP
        OF SWEET, RED WINE;

I HEAR YOUR VOICE
    IN EVERY SONG
        OF LOVE.

IN ALL LIFE'S WARMTH
    I KNOW YOUR PRESENCE;

IN EACH CHILL WIND
    I KNOW YOU'RE GONE.

SOME TIME AGO
    I KNOW YOU LOVED ME –

WHAT SHALL I DO
    FOR TIME TO COME?

NOW AND THEN

NOW AND THEN,

MY THOUGHTS,

ENCOURAGED
    BY A SWEET,
        REMEMBERED KISS,

    BY A LONG
        AWAITED SMILE,

    OR A TENDER TOUCH,

BEGIN,

    IT SEEMS,

TO DANCE
    THROUGH DREAMS

WHICH ONCE
    WERE MINE...

ALONE.

ALONE IN MY OFFICE

THE TEARS OF HEAVEN
STAIN MY OFFICE WINDOW
AND I CAN'T
WIPE THEM AWAY;
FOR THE WINDOW
DOESN'T OPEN
AND THE SUN
HAS GONE FROM DAY.

I CAN SEE
THE LIFELESS RIVER
IN THE DISTANCE,
COLD AND GRAY;
I CAN HEAR THE DIN
OF METROPOLIS...
A MONOTONY
AT PLAY.

I'VE CLOSED
MY OFFICE DOOR;
BUT WHY...
I DO NOT KNOW;
MY PHONE IS SLEEPING
QUIETLY...
THE LIGHTS
I'VE TURNED DOWN LOW.

AND LIKE MY HEART,
I WAIT ALONE
FOR A SIGN OF LIFE
RETURNING...

PLEASE SIGNAL ME,
DEAR GOD,
TO QUELL
MY DESPERATE YEARNING.

YESTERDAY I SAW THE RIVER

YESTERDAY,
I SAW THE RIVER,
CLEAR AND FRESH
AND BLUE;

TODAY,
A HAZE BETWEEN US
STANDS...
A VEIL OF FEARS...
AND DOUBTS
UNTRUE!

I KNOW NOT WHY
THE DREADFUL HAND
SET ON MY SIGHT
A LIMIT NEW;

I ONLY KNOW
THAT 'TIL IT'S GONE,
MY EYES
CANNOT
THE RIVER
VIEW!

THE MATTER OF AGE

I COULD NOT BE
SO SELFISH
AND DISHONEST
AS TO TELL YOU
YOU ARE WRONG;
YOUR CAPACITY
AND NEED
TO GIVE,
TO LOVE,
TO SHARE,
TO CARE FOR
ARE FAR TOO GREAT
FOR ONLY ME;
BUT I COULD NOT
BEGIN AGAIN
BRINGING NEW LIFE
INTO THE WORLD
DESPITE
THE BEAUTY,
JOY
AND LOVE
IT BROUGHT ME.

IT'S SAD,
I KNOW,
BUT JUST AS TRUE;
AND YOU,
IN THE BEAUTY
OF YOUR LOVING
YOUTH,
SHOULD NOT
BE SO DEPRIVED.

I WILL ALWAYS
LOVE YOU…

I HOPE
YOU KNOW THAT.

THE DAY IN THE PARK

I DREAMED A DREAM LAST NIGHT:
WE STOLE AN AFTERNOON AND SPENT
IT IN THE PARK; AND AS WE LENT
OUR EYES TO SEEK A SIGHT
FOR US TO SIT AND GAZE
UPON LOVE'S DOMAIN, WE WALKED THROUGH
SPRINGTIME'S FLORAL PATTERNS FEW
AMID THE SUN'S WARM RAYS;

THE SPOT I SOUGHT WAS HIGH
UPON A STURDY VACANT ROCK,
A BOULDER LARGE AND GRAY; A LOCK
OF LONG, DARK HAIR A SIGH
OF GENTLE BREEZE DID PLACE
ACROSS YOUR BROW AND SOFT EYES
BUT COULD NOT FOR A MOMENT DISGUISE
THE BEAUTY IN YOUR FACE;

I BENT SLIGHTLY, THE STRANDS OF YOUR HAIR
TO BRUSH AWAY; AND AS I TOUCHED
YOUR LOVELINESS SO SOFT, SO TOUCHED
WAS I THAT IN MY HANDS
A COUNTENANCE SO RARE
I PLACED, I JUST COULD NOT REFRAIN
FROM SHOWERING YOU WITH LIGHT RAIN
OF KISSES EVERYWHERE;

OUR CHEMISTRY WAS SUCH
THAT GREENER TURNED THE GRASS HOLDING
US ALOFT, PETALS UNFOLDING
ALL AROUND, TELLING MUCH
THE TALE OF LOVING YOU;
AND AS CONTINUED WE OUR STROLL
TO MOUNTAINTOP, WITHOUT CONTROL,
FUSED OUR HEARTS...ONE FROM TWO;

FROM ON HIGH WE PERCHED SO
LIKE HEAVENLY BIRDS, SPIRITS FREE
AS ONLY LOVERS TRUE COULD BE;
POOR LIFE WE WATCHED BELOW,
NOT UNLIKE WING-CLIPPED DOVE
UNABLE FROM UNBEING FLY
AND WEAVE GAYLY THROUGH TREE AND SKY,
LIKE US, ON WINGS OF LOVE;

WITH IMPUNITY I
DEVOURED WITH EYES AND LIPS YOUR FACE,
THE GIFT OF NATURE...BY GOD'S GRACE
ALONE; WITHOUT A CRY
OF ANGER OR FATEFUL
ASKANT GLANCE, PERMISSIVELY HE
WATCHED, KNOWING THAT MY LOVE WOULD BE
EVER TRUE AND GRATEFUL;

THE HOURS PASSED, CARESSES
AND KISSES FILLED, IDYLLIC DAY
OF GLORIOUS LOVE GIVING WAY...
TIME'S URGENT CALL PRESSES
TO BE HEARD AND HEEDED...
AND WILL BE...DESPITE THE YEARNING
OF OUR HEARTS DISTRAUGHT IN LEARNING
ALL TIME OUR LOVE NEEDED;

WE LEFT THE PARK; GOODBYE,
WE KISSED, OUR LIPS PARTING DELAYED
NOT ENOUGH...WE'D NOT NOW BE SWAYED
TO BELIEVING A LIE:
THAT IF WE'D EVER PART,
WE COULD CONTINUE AS BEFORE
THIS DREAM FOREVERMORE
WAS EVER IN OUR HEART;

THEN, STILL DREAMING, YOU LED
ME TO A PLACE WHERE SIPPED WE WINE
SWEET AS OUR LOVE...YOUR HANDS IN MINE
PRAYER-LIKE I HELD AS FLED
FROM MY MEMORY'S VIEW
ALL DAYS BEFORE THIS DAY...THIS PART
OF MY LIFE'S DREAM FORETOLD...MY HEART
ALL DAYS WOULD ALWAYS BE WITH YOU;

AND THIS I KNEW AS LONG
I GAZED INTO TRUTHFUL, LOVE-FILLED
EYES SO WARM AGLOW...ANGELS MILLED
ABOUT YOU, SINGING LOVE'S SWEET SONG
SOFTLY IN YOUR VOICE...NONE
IN ALL GOD'S TIME WILL EVER BE
GRANTED SUCH BEAUTY GRANTED THEE...
ALL BEAUTY...ALL IN ONE;

IMPATIENT TIME...WILLING
NOT TO WAIT EVEN FOR US, ROSE...
MY DREAM TO BRING TO SUDDEN CLOSE...
NOT UNLIKE CHILD-KILLING...
NO CHOICE BUT TO OBEY,
WE LEFT FOR HOME LIKE SHEEP IN HERD...
SO GRIM IN THOUGHT, HARDLY A WORD
PASSED AS ENDED OUR DAY;

WHEN LOVE SO RARE IS FOUND,
LIKE JEWELS IN THE SEA, RAINBOWS
END, THEN LOST, THE LOVER'S HEART KNOWS
PAIN ONLY WITHOUT BOUND...
THIS DREAM, LIKE AN EARTHQUAKE
TEARING ME APART AS I KNEW
IT WOULD...

THIS DREAM OF LOVING YOU
FROM WHICH I CANNOT WAKE.

SILENT PARTNER

I WAKE UP EVERY MORNING
TO A COLD AND EMPTY ROOM
'CAUSE YOU'VE GONE HOME TO YOUR FAM'LY...
LEAVING ME TO SLEEP ALONE!
MY MIRROR CALLS ME NAMES
I NEVER THOUGHT I WAS BEFORE;
I HURT SO BAD...AND GET SO MAD...
THAT BABY, I CAN'T FAKE IT...
I CAN'T TAKE IT ANYMORE!

YOU'RE JUST LIKE A SILENT PARTNER
WITH A VERY SECRET PLAN...
ALWAYS HIDING IN THE SHADOWS...
TAKING EVERYTHING YOU CAN!

SILENT PARTNER...HIDDEN FEELINGS...
LOVE IN SILENCE SOON WILL DIE...
SILENT PARTNER...SECRET LOVER...
I DON'T WANT TO LIVE A LIE!

YOU TELL ME THAT YOU LOVE ME;
THAT SOON YOU'LL BE ALL MINE;
YOU'LL LET HIM KNOW...
HE'LL LET YOU GO...
BUT, BABY, YOU'VE BEEN LYING...
YOU'VE BEEN LYING ALL THE TIME!
I DON'T WANT A SILENT PARTNER
IN MY BED OR IN MY LIFE!
BE AS SILENT AS YOU WANT TO...
BUT NOW I'M TELLING YOU THAT IT'S TIME...

"JUST GO HOME…GO TO YOUR HUSBAND!
DON'T TELL ME THAT YOU LOVE ME;
DON'T LOOK INTO MY EYES…
JUST READ MY LIPS…DON'T TRY TO KISS THEM…
'CAUSE, BABY, NOW THEY'RE TALKIN'…
AND THEY'RE TELLING YOU GOODBYE!!!

I'M WORTH MUCH MORE THAN HALF YOUR LOVE…
NOT SOME ADVENTURE OUT OF SIGHT!
I'LL WAIT FOR SOMEONE FREE TO LOVE ME…
EVERY DAY…
AND THROUGH THE NIGHT!

RETURN TO MARYLAND

I'M GOING TO RETURN
TO MARYLAND,
SOMEDAY –

TO BE WITH YOU
AGAIN –
EVEN IF
YOU AREN'T THERE!

THE RIVER,

THE RAILROAD TRACKS,

THE TUNNEL –
WITH A KISS
AS DARKNESS ENDS,

THE BOATS
IN THE HARBOR
OF ANNAPOLIS,

THE ROCKS
ALONG THE SHORE...

WILL ALL
BE THERE!

AND I KNOW
I'LL FEEL YOU
IN MARYLAND...
AGAIN...

EVEN IF
YOU AREN'T THERE!

STANDING TREE

MY ARMS REACH OUT
TO YOU
LIKE THE LEAVES OF A TREE
SEEKING THE SUN;

AND SHOULD YOUR LOVE
NOT SHINE ON ME,
NOT FILL MY EMPTY ARMS,
I FEAR THE LEAVES WILL WITHER
AND THE BRANCHES
BARE BECOME.

ALTHOUGH THE TREE
WILL STAND,
IT WILL NOT BE CROWNED
WITH GREEN OF SPRING
OR RED AND GOLD OF FALL;
NO BIRDS WILL PERCH
THEREON TO SING,
OR COURT THEIR MATE,
OR NEST THEIR YOUNG;

NAKED OF BEAUTY,
THE BEAUTY NEAR
WILL NEVER
HEED ITS CALL.

ALTHOUGH THE TREE
WILL STAND,
NO TREE HOUSE
WILL BE BUILT,
NO CHILDREN
CLIMB ITS BOUGH;

IT WON'T SHIELD LOVERS
FROM THE RAIN
OR RUSTLE IN THE BREEZE;

IT NEVER WILL KNOW LIFE AGAIN...
THE WAY IT KNOWS IT
NOW.

YOUR SILENCE CALLS

YOUR SILENCE CALLS,

ITS ELOQUENCE CAPTIVATING

    MY THOUGHTS,

ITS SWEET LILT DRAWING A SMILE

    TO MY LIPS,

ITS TENDER NUANCES WARMING

    MY SOUL;

AND THOUGH THE ECHOS

    OF YOUR LAST GOODBYE

REVERBERATE THROUGH RECOLLECTIONS

    OF PAST REALITY...

MY HOPES DECLINE

DECLINING

AND MY LOVE

NEW HEIGHTS HAS CLIMBED;

FOR DESPITE THE SPOKEN WORD

AND THE CURSIVE PHRASES

ON THE WALLS...

YOUR SILENCE CALLS.

ALWAYS NOW

(A SONG)

I DON'T NEED REMINDERS TO KNOW I STILL LOVE YOU;
I DON'T NEED REMINDERS TO KNOW I STILL CARE;
YOU DON'T HAVE TO TELL ME HOW LONG IT'S BEEN OVER...
YOU'VE ALREADY MADE THAT PERFECTLY CLEAR.

DOESN'T SEEM TO MATTER
THAT YOU'VE FOUND SOMEBODY NEW;
DOESN'T SEEM TO MATTER
YOU DON'T CARE ANYMORE;
YOU DON'T HAVE TO TELL ME
HOW MUCH YOU ONCE LOVED ME...
I'VE ALREADY BEEN DOWN THAT OLD ROAD BEFORE.

BUT I DON'T CARE ABOUT YESTERDAY...
I HAVE THESE FEELINGS NOW!
AND I'LL FEEL THE SAME TOMORROW...
'CAUSE TOMORROW...
    IT WILL BE NOW...

BUT IF THERE EVER WAS A TIME I WAS MISSIN' YOU...
    IT'S NOW...

AND IF THERE EVER WAS A TIME I WAS NEEDIN' YOU...
    IT'S NOW...

AND IF THERE EVER WAS A TIME I WAS LOVIN' YOU...
    IT'S NOW...

BUT THEN AGAIN, IT'S ALWAYS NOW...ISN'T IT?

THE KINGDOM

WITH TIME HER SPAN
AND ALL HER PLAYHOUSE,
THE CHILD-MOTHER,
PRECOCIOUSLY INVENTIVE,
DEMURELY SADISTIC,
HEAVENLY MISCHIEVOUS,
CONCEIVED A KINGDOM
OF FANTASY
OVER WHICH ALL HER BEAUTY
REIGNED,
PROTECTED BY THE ARMY
OF MORTALS
SERVING HER WITH UNSEEING
FAITH
AND THE WILLINGNESS
TO FIGHT TO THE DEATH
FOR HER HONOR
AND FAVOR.

ALWAYS THREATENED
BUT NEVER DEFEATED,
HER SUPREMACY
MAINTAINED
THROUGH THE MOST
ARDUOUS BATTLES
AND CIVIL STRIFE
BY THE INEXPLICABLE AWE
OF HER GRACE,
THE INCREDIBLE
COMMAND OF HER SILENCE,

THE INCOMPARABLE
REWARD
OF HER APPROVING
SMILE,
THE LURE
OF THE HOMEFIRE
IN HER EYES,
THE EUPHORIC
DREAM
OF HER GRATEFUL
KISS...
WHICH CAME BUT ONCE...
AND, IN A MOMENT,
DIED!

POEMS OF LOVE, LIFE & RELATIONSHIPS

POEMS II

SEEKING LOVE...AGAIN

I AWAIT YOUR COMING

NOT GIVEN

TO FORTHRIGHT

EXPRESSION

OR DRAMATIC

DEMONSTRATION

OF CHERISHED

THOUGHTS,

I AWAIT YOUR COMING

INTO MY BEING

TO KNOW

THE SWEETNESS

AND BEAUTY

I HAVE

PREPARED

FOR YOU...

IN MY

GARDEN

OF LOVE.

IF I COULD

IF I COULD

CONVERSE

WITH

FATE,

TALK

TO CHANCE,

NEGOTIATE

WITH,

OR

UTTER

EVEN A WORD,

TO DESTINY,

I WOULD

SPEAK

YOUR NAME.

NO LIES

(FROM A SONG)

THERE CAN'T BE LIES,
IF YOU WANT ME TO LOVE YOU;
THERE CAN'T BE LIES...
THERE IS NO COMPROMISE!
I'D FIND YOUR LIES...
DON'T TRY TO HIDE THEM;

I'D SEE THEM HIDING
IN YOUR EYES!

I KNOW HOW MUCH
YOU WANT MY LOVING;
I KNOW HOW MUCH...THAT'S NO SURPRISE.
MY LOVE IS SURE A PRIZE WORTH WINNING...

BUT SURE OF LOSING
WITH YOUR LIES!

THERE CAN'T BE LIES...
NO LIES!...NO LIES!
DON'T TRY TO LOVE ME
IN DISGUISE;
THERE CAN'T BE LIES...

NO LIES!...NO LIES!
THEY POISON LOVE...
WHICH SOON WILL DIE!

REALLY THERE

I MUST FIND SOMEONE

WHO REALLY UNDERSTANDS

ME...

SOMEONE WHO KNOWS

WHAT I REALLY

THINK,

WHAT I REALLY

BELIEVE,

WHAT I REALLY

WANT,

WHAT I REALLY

NEED,

WHAT I REALLY

FEEL –

AND IS REALLY DESIROUS

OF ACCEPTING

ME

FOR WHO AND WHAT

I REALLY AM...

AND LOVING ME FOR IT.

SELF DEFEAT

IT HAS OCCURED

TO ME

THAT MY ALLOWING

YOU TO KNOW

HOW DESPERATE

I AM

TO LOVE...

AND BE LOVED

MAY VERY WELL

PRECLUDE BOTH!

VERIFICATION

I JUST HAD DINNER

ALONE...

IN A CHINESE RESTAURANT

IN MIDTOWN...

MY FORTUNE COOKIE

WAS EMPTY,

TOO!

GOT TO SEE YOU AGAIN

(A SONG)

I NEVER REALLY LIKED HAVIN' TO SAY GOODBYE;
BUT I ALWAYS DID, SOMEHOW...AND IT WAS FINE;
    THIS TIME, THOUGH, WITH YOU,
        FOR THE VERY FIRST TIME...I CRIED...
    I DON'T KNOW WHY...I JUST CRIED.

I NEVER REALLY DREAMED OF FALLIN' IN LOVE AGAIN...
THOUGHT IT COULDN'T HAPPEN...AND THAT WAS FINE;
    THIS TIME, THOUGH, WITH YOU,
        ALL THE PASSION I'VE HELD...DEEP INSIDE...
        RUSHED RIGHT TO MY HEART...CAME ALIVE.

THE WHOLE WORLD SEEMED SO EMPTY
WHEN THE NIGHT SWEPT IN THE DAY
    LIKE THE INSIDE OF MY BODY
        HAD BEEN SUDDENLY SWEPT AWAY.
I PROBABLY WON'T EVEN TELL YOU THIS
    IF I DO SEE YOU AGAIN...
        AT LEAST UNTIL...I KNOW FOR SURE...
    YOU WON'T EVER LEAVE AGAIN!

GOT TO SEE YOU AGAIN...FIND OUT WHAT I'M FEELIN'...
I NEVER CRIED BEFORE FROM ANYONE'S GOODBYE.
GOT TO SEE YOU AGAIN...STOP MY HEAD FROM REELIN'...

I'LL NEVER CRY AGAIN FROM ANYONE'S GOODBYE.

THE SECRET IN YOUR EYES

(A SONG)

THERE'S A SECRET
IN YOUR EYES
THAT'S CAPTURED
MY IMAGINATION
WITH A STORY
TO BE TOLD
OF LOVE
AND SWEET SENSATION;

THERE'S A SECRET
IN YOUR EYES
AND YOU WANT
TO SET IT FREE...
TO GIVE THE LOVE
YOU HAVE TO GIVE
AND BE
WHAT YOU
CAN BE;

THERE'S A SECRET
IN YOUR EYES
THAT MUST BE SHARED
WITH SOMEONE NEW...

SOMEONE
WHO UNDERSTANDS...
LIKE ME –

WHO HAS THAT SECRET,
TOO!

YOU AND I

LIKE SHIPS
PASSING IN THE NIGHT,
CARESSED
BY THE SAME
WARM BREEZE,
BUT DARING NOT
TO TOUCH;

DRAWN
TO PORTS
A SEA APART,
PROBABLY
NEVER
TO MEET
AGAIN;

LIKE THE SEA
AND THE SKY,
MEETING ONLY
IN THE UNTOUCHABLE
HORIZON –
AN OPTICAL ILLUSION
OF OUR LIMITED
VIEW;

AN IRONIC PAIR
IN NATURE'S DESIGN...

THE SINE-QUA-NON
OF LIFE ITSELF...

IN OUR ETERNAL
SEPARATION.

WHAT MIGHT HAVE BEEN

I WAS IN A RESTAURANT...

SHE LOOKED AT ME

FROM ACROSS THE ROOM...

AND SMILED –

A WARM,

PRETTY...

VERY INVITING

SMILE.

I ACKNOWLEDGED...

AND SMILED BACK.

BUT WHY

DID I LET IT END...

THERE?

IN QUIET DESPERATION

IN QUIET DESPERATION
    WAITS MY HEART
    FOR LOVE TO BEGIN...
    MY LIFE TO START...
        EXISTING ON HOPE,
        BREATHING IN PRAYER,
        WANTING FOR NAUGHT
        BUT YOU TO APPEAR.

IN QUIET DESPERATION
    WAITS MY HEART
    FOR FLOWERS TO BLOOM,
        A BEE'S STING TO SMART
        LONGING TO FEEL,
        YEARNING TO BE,
        PLEADING TO GOD
        THAT YOU COME TO ME.

IN QUIET DESPERATION
    WAITS MY HEART
    FOR DARKNESS TO END,
    BLACK CLOUDS TO PART,
        SEEING BY DREAMS,
        LEARNING TO STRIVE
        REQUIRING ONLY
        YOUR LOVE TO SURVIVE.

IN QUIET DESPERATION
    WAITS MY HEART
    FOR ITS ACHE TO CEASE,
  A HALT TO ITS PINE;
    FOR UNTIL THE LOVE
    THAT'S YOURS IS MINE,
      IN QUIET DESPERATION
      WAITS MY HEART.

HAVING NOT YOUR LOVE

HAVING NOT YOUR LOVE...

I CAN SEE NAUGHT BUT EMPTY SKY,

I CANNOT HEAR A BABY'S CRY...

NO TASTE IS THERE IN CHERRY PIE....

HAVING NOT YOUR LOVE.

HAVING NOT YOUR LOVE...

NO FRAGRANCE HAS A FLOWERED PLAIN,

I CANNOT FEEL THE GENTLE RAIN...

MY SENSES ARE FOR USE IN VAIN...

HAVING NOT YOUR LOVE.

IF YOUR LOVE

YOU FAIL

TO GIVE...

I'LL NEVER BEGIN

TO REALLY

LIVE.

ENCOUNTER

AN UNINTENDED

ENCOUNTER,

A CAPTURED

GLANCE;

SWEET

ROMANCE

IN DREAMS

SET ASIDE;

FATE'S

REMINDER

OF MEMORIES

TO BE...

OR,

JUST A SPREE

OF

UNSPENT

LOVE.

DON'T LAUGH AT ME

DON'T LAUGH AT ME

    WHEN TEARS SWELL IN MY EYES...

FOR WANTING YOU TO LOVE

BRINGS ONLY PAIN

    AND HOPELESS CRIES...

DON'T LAUGH AT ME!

    DON'T LAUGH AT ME!

DON'T LAUGH AT ME

    AS LOVED ONES OFTEN DO

'CAUSE MY WHOLE LIFE

    DEPENDS ON LOVING YOU...

DON'T LAUGH AT ME!

    DON'T LAUGH AT ME!

DON'T LAUGH AT ME!

    DON'T LAUGH AT ME!

PLEASE, MY LOVE,

    DON'T LAUGH AT ME!

DID YOU EVER NOTICE...?

DID YOU EVER NOTICE...?

NO –

I GUESS

YOU NEVER DID...

WHAT A SHAME!

LOVE

WOULD HAVE BEEN

SO BEAUTIFUL!

CONFLICT

THOUGHTS,
INSTILLED
IN THE TRANQUIL
MEMORIES
OF YOUR TENDER

KISS;

DREAMS,
IMPETUOUSLY
CONJURED
BY YOUR
FORTHRIGHT

LOVING,

CHALLENGE
REALITY –

PRESSING
INCESSANTLY

FOR
RECOGNITION.

BEWARE

SLOWLY WEAVING

    THROUGH ENCHANTING MEMORIES

        OF UNTOLD MOMENTS

SET ASIDE

    BY DREAMS

        UNDREAMED,

MY THOUGHTS,

    DELIRIOUS

        WITH VISIONS

OF YOUR BODY

    RESPONDING

        TO MY KISS,

DRIFT SENSUOUSLY

    INTO MY BEING.

A PLEA

PERHAPS,
I'M JUST
IN LOVE
WITH LOVE –

I'VE CONSIDERED THAT
IN MOMENTS
OF DISAPPOINTMENT –

BUT THEN,
PERHAPS,
I DO HAVE
MORE
TO GIVE.

PLEASE
HELP ME
FIND

THE ANSWER.

AFTERTHOUGHT

LOVE,

IN AFTERTHOUGHT –

A CONSTANT

ON

MY MIND!

ON RARE OCCASION

WHEN,

ON RARE OCCASION,

I CAN THINK

THOUGHTS

OTHER THAN

OF YOU,

MY MIND BEGINS

TO RACE

LIKE HELL...

TOO SOON

I CAN'T

BE THROUGH!

A DECISION

IT'S BEEN SO LONG
SINCE I'VE EXPERIENCED THIS FEELING
OF TOTAL INNER WARMTH...
I MUST ADMIT
I'M CONFUSED –
    EVEN FRIGHTENED –
HER YOUTHFUL LOVELINESS,
    SO REAL,
PORTEND THE BEAUTIFUL WOMAN...
AT TWENTY-THREE -
    ABOUT TO BE;

AND I'M FRUSTRATED
BY THE PROBABILITIES
THAT, ON THE ONE HAND –
FOR HER,
    I'M MUCH TOO EARLY;
AND, ON THE OTHER HAND –
FOR ME,
    SHE'S MUCH TOO LATE!

AM I WRONG
IN WANTING
TO PURSUE THIS ADVENTURE?

I KNOW
HOW MUCH I HAVE TO GIVE;
BUT WILL MY GIVING
    TAKE AWAY TOO MUCH?
WILL MY TAKING
    NOT GIVE BACK ENOUGH?

PERHAPS,
I'M JUST UNDERESTIMATING
    BOTH OF US –
OR…
ONLY HER.

I THINK IT'S WORTH A TRY –
    IT SHOULD BE!

I WILL!

CHANGING MOOD

IT'S AMAZING

HOW QUICKLY

AND EASILY

MY MOOD

CAN CHANGE

SIMPLY

BECAUSE

YOU SMILED

AT ME.

CAN YOU

IMAGINE

WHAT A HUG

WOULD DO...

OR,

PERISH

THE THOUGHT,,,

A KISS?

POEMS OF LOVE, LIFE & RELATIONSHIPS

POEMS III

LOVE FOUND

POEMS OF LOVE, LIFE & RELATIONSHIPS

POEMS III

LOVE FOUND

WHAT A WAY TO START THE DAY

(A SONG)

IT WAS JUST ANOTHER DAY...
WHERE NOTHING REALLY HAPPENS;
BUT THEN I SAW YOU TURN THE CORNER
AND YOUR FACE CAME INTO VIEW;

I THOUGHT I MUST BE DREAMING,
YOU LOOKED TOO GOOD TO BE TRUE...
BUT THERE YOU WERE...IN REAL LIFE...
AND RIGHT THERE ON THAT VERY SPOT...
I FELL IN LOVE WITH YOU!

WHAT A WAY TO START THE DAY –
GET IT OFF THE GROUND...
SEE YOUR DREAM...
FIND YOUR LOVE...
TURN YOUR LIFE AROUND!

I JUST WANTED TO BE HAPPY...
FIND SOMEONE TO LOVE ME...
BUT WAS ALWAYS MISSING SOMETHING
'TIL I FOUND IT ALL IN YOU!

NEVER THOUGHT I'D GET SO LUCKY
TO HAVE FOUND THE ONLY YOU...
BUT HERE YOU ARE...IN REAL LIFE...
AND EVERY MINUTE OF MY LIFE...
I'LL BE IN LOVE WITH YOU!

THE GREATEST TIME
IS LOVE'S BEGINNING
WHEN EVERTHING'S BRAND NEW...
WHEN EVERY DAY
THERE'S ONLY WINNING...

THERE'S ONLY ME AND YOU!

YOUR KISS

WITH DELIBERATE
SLOWNESS
I DRANK
YOUR KISS...
MY TONGUE,
FONDLING
YOURS,
SWIMMING
LUXURIOUSLY
THROUGH AN OCEAN
OF RAPTUROUS
JUICES,
REACHING
WITH A SIGH
ITS OWN
HIGH
AS I LONG DELAYED
EACH SWALLOW,
BRINGING
YOUR BEING
IN,
DOWN,
THROUGHOUT MINE,
PERMEATING
MY SOUL,
MY SPIRIT...

THE VERY
ESSENCE
OF MY
EXISTENCE.

HEART TO HEART

(A SONG)

TIME PASSES BY...
OUR ROADS DON'T SEEM TO CROSS;
WE'VE BOTH BEEN SO ALONE SO LONG...
CAN'T FIND THE FEELINGS LOVE HAS LOST;

BUT MY HEART'S BEEN ALWAYS WITH YOU
IN OUR FRIENDSHIP FROM THE START;
NOW IT'S TIME WE GET TOGETHER...
GET TOGETHER...HEART TO HEART.

DAYS LINGER ON...
THE NIGHTS DON'T SEEM TO END;
WE CALL TO CALM EACH OTHER DOWN...
CAN'T HEAR THE MESSAGE HEAVEN SENT;

BUT MY HEART'S BEEN ALWAYS WITH YOU
IN OUR FRIENDSHIP FROM THE START;
SO, IT'S TIME TO GET TOGETHER –
GET TOGETHER HEART TO HEART.

THE GREATER LOVE WILL ALWAYS GROW
WHEN FRIENDSHIP IS THE SEED...
AS THE ROOTS OF ALL OUR FEELINGS
WILL BE STRONGER THAN
THE STRONGEST WIND
    OF ANY PASSING NEED!

AND MY HEART'S BEEN ALWAYS WITH YOU
IN OUR FRIENDSHIP FROM THE START;
SO, IT'S TIME WE GET TOGETHER –
GET TOGETHER HEART TO HEART.

YOUR VOICE WITHIN THE BREEZE

YOUR VOICE WITHIN THE BREEZE
SPEAKS SOFTLY,

YOUR EYES
AMONG THE STARS
GLOW WARM,

YOUR PETAL FINGERS
UNFOLD
LIFE GAYLY,

YOUR LIPS
IN SWEET, RED WINE
RUNS LOVE;

YOUR SMILE
TURNS ON
THE SPRING,

YOUR KISS,
THE SUMMER'S DAY;

YOUR BEAUTY LIVES
IN ALL LIFE'S BEAUTY,

YOUR LOVE
IN ALL
LOVE'S LOVE.

GLAD

I SAID I WAS GLAD
    I CALLED YOU;

YOU SAID YOU WERE GLAD
    I CALLED YOU, TOO;

I SAID I WAS EVEN MORE GLAD
    THAT YOU WERE GLAD
        I CALLED YOU...

YOU LAUGHED!

IT WAS FUNNY -

IN ITS SILLINESS –
    ALL THOSE GLADS;

BUT THEY WERE SINCERE
    AND WARM
        AND, OH, SO WELCOME;

AND THEY REOPENED A DOOR
   I THOUGHT FOREVER CLOSED...

I ALMOST HATE TO SAY IT,

   BUT, I CAN'T BEGIN TO TELL YOU

      HOW GLAD I AM

         FOR ALL THOSE GLADS.

FALLING IN LOVE

TO CONFUSE

FALLING IN LOVE

WITH ALREADY BEING THERE

COULD MAKE THE FALLING FATAL

AND THE FEELINGS DISAPPEAR;

THE ONLY TIME

YOU'RE REALLY IN LOVE

IS AFTER THE FALL...

AND ALL THE FANTASIES

OF FALLING

BECOME SWEET MEMORIES,

NOT OF SOMETHING

LOST,

BUT OF SOMETHING

ALWAYS

WITH YOU!

MY LOVE FOR YOU WILL BE

MY LOVE FOR YOU
WILL BE
EVER DEEPER
THAN THE SEA,

EYES ONLY FOR YOUR
BEAUTY
AND ELEGANCE
TO SEE,

LIPS WANTING ONLY
YOUR PRECIOUS
LIPS
TO KISS,

HANDS, FOR A MOMENT,
YOUR SOFTNESS
NOT
TO MISS,

ARMS FOR
YOUR BODY
EVER CLOSE IN MINE
TO HOLD,

BODY ALL AROUND
YOU
AS A SHIELD
AGAINST THE COLD,

LIFE WITHIN YOUR
WARMTH
BRINGING ECSTACY
SO HIGH…
I'LL HAVE BUT ONE
DESIRE –
TO LOVE YOU
'TIL I DIE.

THE FEAR OF LOSING YOU

THE FEAR OF LOSING YOU

    PRESSES ALL TOO HEAVILY

        ON MY MIND

            THE TIME I NEED YOU MOST;

AND THE TIME

    I NEED YOU MOST

        IS WHEN THE MOST

            I FEAR

    IS THE FEAR

        OF LOSING YOU

LIKE TIME ALONE

(A SONG)

SOMEWHERE IN TIME, THE DAY WILL COME
WHEN GENTLE RAIN WILL CEASE TO FALL
WHEN SHINING SUN WILL DIM...
WHEN BREATH OF LIFE WILL LEAVE US ALL
TO SING NOT SONG NOR HYMN...

SOMEWHERE IN TIME, THE DAY WILL COME
WHEN ALL THE BIRDS WILL CEASE TO FLY
WHEN GOLD WILL LOSE ITS GLOW...
WHEN RIVERS DEEP AND STREAMS NEARBY
WILL EBB AND NO MORE FLOW...

SOMEWHERE IN TIME, THE DAY WILL COME
WHEN FIRES OF PASSION WILL CEASE TO BURN
WHEN TEARS FROM EYES WON'T RUN...
WHEN SUMMER LIKE ITS LEAVES WILL TURN
FROM GREEN TO BROWN TO NONE...

THOUGH EVERYTHING MAY CHANGE
AND TRUTH BECOMES A LIE...
MY LOVE FOR YOU...LIKE TIME ALONE,
WILL NEVER, EVER DIE!

IT WILL NEVER EVER DIE!

NO DOUBT ABOUT IT

NO DOUBT ABOUT IT...
FRIENDSHIPS COME AND FRIENDSHIPS GO;
NO DOUBT ABOUT IT...
FEW EXCEPTIONS, AS YOU KNOW
NO DOUBT ABOUT IT...
ACQUAINTANCES FLASH OFF AND ON
NO DOUBT ABOUT IT...
HERE A MOMENT, THEN THEY'RE GONE!

FLIRTATIONS ARE LIKE RAINDROPS...
KINDA TICKLE AS THEY TOUCH...
THEN QUICKLY DISAPPEAR;
INFATUATIONS SOMETIMES LAST...
A WEEK...A MONTH ...
SOMETIMES A YEAR

BUT, LOVE'S NOT LIKE THE REST...
IT WILL ALWAYS FEEL BRAND NEW...
THERE'S JUST NO DOUBT ABOUT IT...
LOVE WILL LAST OUR WHOLE LIFE THROUGH!

NO DOUBT ABOUT IT...
LOVE WAS MADE FOR YOU AND ME;
NO DOUBT ABOUT IT...
YOU AND ME WILL ALWAYS BE
TOGETHER...
FOREVER!

WALK WITH ME

WALK WITH ME,
MY LOVE,
THROUGH A DREAM
I'M GOING TO HAVE...
IT WILL BE ABOUT A LIFETIME –
YOURS AND MINE
WHICH WILL BE FILLED
WITH LOVE
AND BEAUTY...
AND HAPPINESS
UNTOLD,
WITH BIRDS
ALWAYS SINGING
AND FLOWERS
ALWAYS IN BLOOM.
PLEASE WALK WITH ME,
MY LOVE...
PLEASE WALK WITH ME.

WE'LL STROLL
THROUGH THE HEAVENS,
GATHERING STARS
ALONG THE WAY;
AND AS I PLACE THEM
IN YOUR HAIR,
THEY WILL GAIN
ETERNAL LIGHT;
AND THEY'LL SPARKLE
EVER BRIGHTER
AS ON THEY TAKE

THE LUSTRE OF YOUR FACE;
YET THEIR GLOW
WILL HAVE A LOVING WARMTH
AS THEY EMULATE
YOUR EYES.

PLEASE WALK WITH ME,
MY LOVE...
PLEASE WALK WITH ME.
WE'LL PRANCE
ACROSS THE VALLEYS...
TIPTOEING
FROM MOUNTAIN PEAK
TO MOUNTAIN PEAK
IN EFFORTLESS STRIDES;

WE'LL DANCE
ATOP THE TREES
SO LIGHTLY
NOT EVEN
THE MOST TIMID BIRDS
WILL TAKE NOTE;

AND WE'LL SKIP ACROSS
THE OCEANS...
MAKING RIPPLES
OUT OF TIDAL WAVES;

AND HERE AND THERE
WE'LL STOP TO REST
AND SIT UPON
A CLOUD
WHILE WE GAZE ABOUT
IN ALL DIRECTIONS
AT OUR TREASURES
EVERYWHERE;

WE'LL LIE UPON A BED
OF MOONBEAMS,
A PILLOW OF SUNRAYS
BENEATH OUR HEAD...
AND A BLANKET
OF LOVE
TO COVER US;
PLEASE WALK WITH ME,
MY LOVE...
PLEASE WALK WITH ME.

WE'LL BE CONSUMED
BY OUR LOVE;
AND AS OUR LIPS
AND BODIES BLEND
INTO ONE,
ECSTACY

WILL PERMEATE
OUR BEING,
JOY
WILL RUN
THROUGH OUR VEINS,
ANGER
WILL DISSIPATE,
JEALOUSY
EVAPORATE,
HATRED
WILL BECOME
NONEXISTENT...
TIME WILL STOP
AND PAIN
WILL DIE;
PLEASE WALK WITH ME,
MY LOVE...
PLEASE WALK WITH ME.

WALK WITH ME,
MY LOVE,
THROUGH THIS DREAM
I'M GOING TO HAVE;
FOR THE ESSENCE
OF THE DREAM
IS YOU –
YOUR LOVE
WILL MAKE IT ALL
COME TRUE.

PLEASE WALK WITH ME,
MY LOVE...
PLEASE WALK WITH ME...
TAKE MY HAND,
MY LOVE...
AND WALK WITH ME.

A PROMISE TRUE

IN LIGHT OF THE ABOVE, MY LOVE,
I MAKE THIS PROMISE TRUE:
    NO MATTER WHAT FATE HAS IN STORE,
    I'LL NOT STOP LOVING YOU!

I'LL SEE YOU CLEAR IN HEAVEN'S EYES,
IN CANDLE'S GLOW, IN SPRING'S DESIGNS;
I'LL LOOK FOR YOU AT EVERY TURN,
ON EVERY ROAD – NO MATTER SAY THE SIGNS;
I'LL SEE YOUR FACE IN EVERY GLASS
OF LUSCIOUS, SWEET, RED WINE...
AND DRINK YOUR LIPS SO TENDERLY...
MY LIPS WILL CRY OF THINE;

I'LL HOLD YOU IN MY HANDS
WITH EACH FLOWER THAT I TOUCH,
WITH EACH SNOWFLAKE THAT IN FLIGHT I CATCH...
EACH TIME I PRAY – I PRAY SO MUCH!

I'LL HEAR YOUR VOICE IN SUMMER'S BREEZE,
IN EVERY MOMENT WE'RE APART,
IN EVERY WHISPER OF THE TREES,
IN EVERY BEAT WITHIN MY HEART;

    AS EVERY MOMENT I EXIST,
    EXISTS, MY LOVE, IN YOU;
    YOUR LOVE AND BEAUTY EVERYWHERE
    WILL KEEP THIS PROMISE TRUE!

POEMS OF LOVE, LIFE & RELATIONSHIPS

POEMS IV

FOR THOSE I LOVE
FOR MY WIFE

A STATEMENT OF ABSOLUTE TRUTH
MADE WITH THE FULLEST
KNOWLEDGE
OF ALL ITS MEANINGS,
EXPRESS AND IMPLIED,
WHILE STANDING ON
THE THRESHOLD
OF FOREVER
AFTER COMPLETING
THE COMPUTATION
FOR ETERNITY

I STILL LOVE YOU!

A LITTLE RUBBER DUCK

(FOUND BY MY FUTURE WIFE WHEN
WE WERE FIRST DATING)

WE WERE WALKING IN A PARK,
ALONGSIDE A PRETTY LITTLE POND,
WHEN WE CAME UPON
A LITTLE RUBBER DUCK,
ABANDONED BY A CHILD -
    FOR SOME OTHER CHILD TO FIND -

CAST UPON THE SHORE OF OUR REAL WORLD –
    AN UNNATURAL HABITAT –

JUST WAITING TO BE FOUND -
    AND WAS GENTLY LIFTED BY YOUR WARM,
    LOVING HANDS
    AND HELD CLOSE TO YOUR HEART...

YOU WERE THAT OTHER CHILD
    WHO COULD SEE THE BEAUTY

AND FEEL THE LOVE AND LIFE
    IN NOTHING MORE

THAN A LITTLE RUBBER DUCK...

AND LUCKY ME TO HAVE FOUND
   THAT OTHER CHILD

THAT'S WHEN I KNEW

I WAS IN LOVE WITH YOU.

FOR MY WIFE
ON HER BIRTHDAY

BIRTHDAYS
ARE BEGINNINGS –
BEGINNINGS OF LIFE
AND ALL ITS BEAUTIFUL
OFFERINGS,
INCLUDING
AND ESPECIALLY,
LOVE.

THE BEST
THAT I CAN WISH
FOR YOU
IS THAT YOU ARE ALWAYS
SURROUNDED
BY LOVE,
ENVELOPED
BY LOVE,
SO THAT
IT PERMEATES
YOUR BEING
AND LIVES
FOREVER
INSIDE YOU
WHERE IT WILL GROW
AND THRIVE
IN A HABITAT
MADE FOR LOVE.

PLEASE ACCEPT
MY LOVE
EVEN THOUGH
IN DOING SO
IT BECOMES
YOUR GIFT
TO ME.

ON OUR FIRST ANNIVERSARY

JUNE 8, 1987

IT'S BEEN A YEAR
AND YET IT SEEMS,
AT THE SAME TIME,
A MINUTE
AND FOREVER.

YOU'VE MADE
A DIFFICULT TIME
MORE THAN JUST
TOLERABLE –
YOU'VE MADE IT FEEL EASY.

YOU'VE BRIGHTENED
THE DAYS
WITH YOUR SUNSHINE
AND WARMED
THE NIGHTS
WITH YOUR GLOW.

I LOVE YOU
WITH ALL MY HEART
AND NINETY-NINE PERCENT
OF MY SOUL.

PLEASE PICK UP
MY OPTION
FOR ANOTHER YEAR –
FOR OUR LIFETIME –
IF YOU WILL.

I WOULD MARRY YOU AGAIN

(A SONG FOR OUR 25TH ANNIVERSARY)
(LINK TO YOUTUBE https://www.youtube.com/watch?v=X1fBmSpMv_Q)

IT STILL FEELS LIKE YESTERDAY
WHEN I SAID "I DO" TO YOU...
AND A HUNDRED YEARS FROM NOW,
I'LL STILL LOVE YOU.

ALL THE THINGS THAT WE'VE BEEN THROUGH,
ALL WE'VE SEEN AND HAD TO DO...
WE CAME THROUGH IT ALL SOMEHOW...
AND I STILL LOVE YOU...OH, I STILL LOVE YOU!

I REMEMBER OUR FIRST DATE...I REMEMBER IT WAS LATE...
I REMEMBER IT ALL LIKE IT WAS YESTERDAY,
I REMEMBER OUR FIRST KISS...I REMEMBER IT WAS BLISS...
I REMEMBER NEVER WANTING IT TO END...
I REMEMBER...I REMEMBER...OH, I REMEMBER...

AND THROUGH EVERY PASSING YEAR,
LIFE'S BEEN SO WONDERFUL...
FOR THE NEXT HUNDRED YEARS
I'LL STILL LOVE YOU...

ALL THE SILLY THINGS WE'VE DONE;
ALL THE TIMES WE'VE HAD SUCH FUN...
OH, A HUNDRED YEARS FROM NOW...
I'LL STILL LOVE YOU...OH, I'LL STILL LOVE YOU...

AND I WOULD MARRY YOU AGAIN...IN A HEARTBEAT!
YES, I'D MARRY YOU AGAIN...ANYTIME!
I WOULD MARRY YOU AGAIN...FOR A LIFETIME...
YOU'RE MY SOUL MATE...MY BEST FRIEND...
AND I WANT YOU BY MY SIDE...

'CAUSE I STILL LOVE YOU...I STILL LOVE YOU...
YES, I STILL LOVE YOU.

SHORTNESS IS THE KEY

WE GOT THROUGH
THE FIRST THREE
REGIMENS...
THE FIRST SIX
MONTHS
OF CHEMOTHERAPY;

AND THEN
CAME THE ULTIMATE
CHALLENGE...
THE FINAL
REGIMEN...
AS IF
LOSING
HER BREAST
WAS NOT ENOUGH...
NOW SHE WAS ABOUT
TO LOSE
ALL HER HAIR.

SHE THOUGHT
HER FEMININE
ATTRACTION
WOULD NOW
BE TOTALLY
GONE;

ONE OF HER
CLOSEST FRIENDS
WHO WAS
THERE
TOLD HER
    IT WAS HER BODY...
    SHE SHOULDN'T
    LET ANYONE
    TELL HER
    WHAT TO DO
    WITH IT;

I WANTED TO THROW
THAT FRIEND
OUT THE EIGHTEENTH FLOOR
WINDOW...
DESPITE THE FACT
THAT I LOVED HER...

AFTER ALL,
I WANTED A LIVING WIFE...
NOT A DEAD FEMINIST!

WE'RE THEN
ALL STANDING
THERE,
LOOKING AT HER...
WAITING;

WE'RE NOW
AT THE MOMENT
OF TRUTH...
SHE IS CRYING...
    SHE DOESN'T KNOW
    WHAT TO DO...
THE DOCTORS
AND NURSES
ARE SAYING
    SHE'S GOT
    TO MAKE UP
    HER MIND.

I FIRMLY BELIEVED
WE'VE COME TOO
FAR...
WE CAN'T STOP
NOW!

I'M ANGRY...
I'M CONFUSED...
I'M FEARFUL
I'VE GOT TO DO
    SOMETHING...
I'VE GOT TO SAY
    SOMETHING...
HAVING LOVINGLY
TEASED MY WIFE

ABOUT BEING
SHORT,
I CALLED OUT
TO THE CHIEF
ONCOLOGIST
AND ASKED HIM
IF THE ADRIAMYCIN
MY WIFE
WAS ABOUT TO TAKE
WOULD ALSO MAKE HER
TALLER...
TO WHICH HE REPLIED,
"OF COURSE NOT!"

I IMMEDIATELY ASKED,
"DOES THAT MEAN
SHE'S GOING TO REMAIN
SHORT?"
TO WHICH
HE REPLIED,
"ABSOLUTELY!"

AT THAT MOMENT,
EVERYONE PRESENT,
EXCEPT
MY WIFE AND ME,
LOOKED CONFUSED...

I TOOK HER HAND
AND SAID,
"LET'S GO,"
AND WE WENT
TO THE TREATMENT ROOM.

THAT WAS ALMOST
30 YEARS AGO...
AND, THANK GOD,
MY WIFE
IS STILL
SHORT!

WHEN THE SONG IS OVER

WHEN THE VERSES

ARE ALL OVER

AND THE CHORUSES

ARE DONE,

WHEN WE'VE FOUGHT

THE FINAL BATTLE

AND THE PRIZE

WE SOUGHT

IS WON,

I WILL NOT

BE VERY HAPPY

UNLESS

THROUGHOUT IT ALL,

WE DID IT

ALL TOGETHER,,,

AND TOGETHER,,,

DID IT ALL!

POEMS OF LOVE, LIFE & RELATIONSHIPS

POEMS V

FOR THOSE I LOVE

FOR SPECIAL PEOPLE / SPECIAL OCCASIONS

LITTLE GIRL WITH THE WHITE COAT ON

FOR OUR MALTESE

YOU CAME TO US ON CHRISTMAS EVE...
WE COULDN'T ASK FOR MORE;
YOUR BIG ROUND EYES SO SOFT AND SWEET...
SO EASY TO ADORE!

HEY LITTLE GIRL WITH THE WHITE COAT ON...
WHITE AS SNOW...AND JUST AS BRIGHT;
HEY LITTLE GIRL WITH THE WHITE COAT ON...
WE LOVE YOU THROUGH THE DAY
AND RIGHT ON THROUGH THE NIGHT!

YOU BRING US JOY AND WARMTH AND LOVE...
YOU'RE LIKE THE MORNING LIGHT;
AND WHEN YOU SNUGGLE UP TO US,
THE WORLD JUST SEEMS ALRIGHT!

YOU LOVE TO RUN AND JUMP AND PLAY;
YOU LOVE TO CUDDLE, TOO...
BUT BEST OF ALL, WHEN YOU SHOW YOU CARE...
WE CAN'T STOP LOVING YOU!

MY 25TH HIGH SCHOOL REUNION

ONLY YOU,
EARTH ANGEL,
IN THE STILL OF THE NIGHT
BROUGHT TEARS TO MY EYES
AS THE GIRLS
I USED TO DANCE WITH
SO TENDERLY
EVAPORATED
INTO WHAT SEEMED TO BE
SUDDEN WOMANHOOD.

I KNEW
IT WOULDN'T BE THE SAME,
SO, I JUST LISTENED,
PREFERRING TO DANCE
IN THE MEMORIES
OF BEAUTIFUL TIMES GONE BY,
HOLDING THE WARMTH
THAT BELONGED TO ME,
ALONE,
IN MY AFFAIR TO REMEMBER
WHEN LOVE
WAS A MANY SPLENDORED THING.

THE TEARS AND SMILES
OF NEAR-EXPECTED
AND SOMETIMES EVEN
TOTAL SURPRISES
BURST, LIKE FIREWORKS,

THROUGHOUT THE CELEBRATION,
ALONG WITH
THE OH MY GODS!
I DON'T BELIEVE ITS!
YOU LOOK FANTASTICS!
AND THE INEVITABLE
WHATEVER HAPPENED TO SO-AND-SOS,
INTERSPERSED
WITH CAPSULE VERSIONS
OF OUR TRIALS AND TRIBULATIONS
OVER THE INTERVENING YEARS.

STRANGE,
HOW INSIGNIFICANT
OUR LIVES CAN SEEM
WHEN SPONTANEOUSLY REVIEWED
IN AN ORAL ESSAY
OF THE HOW I SPENT LAST SUMMER TYPE –
IN ONE HUNDRED WORDS – OR LESS.

SLOWLY,
I WAS SHOCKED INTO THE PRESENT
AS, AGAIN AND AGAIN,
THE LOVELY FACES
NEEDED TO BE MATCHED
WITH THE NAMETAGS BELOW,
OR VICE-VERSA;
AND SOME, OF COURSE,

DIDN'T MATCH AT ALL;
MINE, I WAS TOLD, DID...
THAT FELT GOOD.

SOME THINGS
HADN'T CHANGED AT ALL;
I STILL LIKED THE SAME PEOPLE –
SOME LESS, SOME MORE;
I STILL DISLIKED THE SAME PEOPLE –
SOME LESS, SOME MORE;
THE MAIN DIFFERENCE,
SO WELCOME,
WAS GETTING TO KNOW
AND FEELING GOOD
ABOUT SOME PEOPLE
I SOMEHOW MISSED BEFORE.

OF THE FORTY-TWO
CENTAURS,
ONLY ABOUT SIX OF US
SHOWED UP;
AND OF THE DOZEN
CENTAURETTES,
ONLY TWO OR THREE WERE THERE;
I RECALL SEEING ONLY ONE
CELESTIAL –
A MAJOR DISAPPOINTMENT –
THEY WERE, AFTER ALL,
QUITE LOVELY.

ACHIEVEMENTS
HAD BEEN MADE
AND GOALS REACHED
AS EVIDENCED
BY THE MANY CAREERS
BEING FOLLOWED
IN ACCORDANCE
WITH THE ASPIRATIONS
STATED IN THE YEARBOOK –
AURORA
JUNE, 1959
TJHS.

WHAT A GREAT CLASS!
WHAT GREAT TIMES!
OUR NAIVETE
SO GROWN-UP THEN –
SO CHARMING NOW;
THE URGENT IMPORTANCE
OF EACH MOMENT
TURNING OUT TO BE
NOTHING MORE IMPORTANT
THAN THE MOMENTS
THEMSELVES –
AND NOTHING LESS.

AND WHEN I WENT
TO WASH UP,

I REALIZED WITH FINALITY
IT WAS ALL IN THE PAST –
NOBODY WAS SMOKING...
IN THE BATHROOM.

THE PARTY,
ALL TOO EXPECTEDLY,
LIKE THE WONDERFUL LIFETIME
IT SUMMARIZED,
CAME TO A SUDDEN CLOSE
WITH WARM, HESITANT
GOODBYES,
EXCHANGES OF TELEPHONE NUMBERS
AND PROMISES
TO KEEP IN TOUCH –
SOME EVEN SINCERE.

BUT THEN,
FOR ME,
IN A NEAR-FINAL MOMENT,
CAME THE CROWNING GLORY
OF THE ENTIRE EVENT:

AFTER
TWENTY-FIVE YEARS,
I FINALLY
GOT A DATE
WITH A TWIRLER!

MY BABY

SWEETNESS AND JOY
CAME HOME LAST NIGHT,
HER MID-WINTER VACATION
HAVING COME TO AN END,
HER SMILING FACE LIGHTLY TANNED,
HER BUBBLY "HI DAD!"
WARMING MY HEART.

I MISSED HER!

I MISSED HER
EVEN MORE SO THIS TIME
AS I REALIZED
THAT THIS TIME NEXT YEAR
WOULD BE ONE OF THE SHORT
PERIODS OF TIME
THAT I WOULD GET TO SEE HER,
AND ALL THE OTHER TIMES
SHE WOULD BE AWAY –
FIRST, AT COLLEGE;
THEN, AT LIFE.

THE TURNAROUND
WAS JUST AROUND
THE CORNER;
THE BREAKS FOR HER
WOULD NOW BECOME
BREAKS FOR ME

(ALBEIT OF A DIFFERENT KIND) -
AND EVEN THOSE
WOULD DIMINISH
IN NUMBER AND EXTENT
AS SHE CONTINUED
WITH DEVELOPING
HER OWN LIFE,
HER OWN STYLE,
HER OWN
EVERYTHING...

OF COURSE I UNDERSTAND
THAT THAT
IS WHAT IT'S ALL ABOUT
AND,
THAT'S
THE WAY
IT SHOULD BE;
BUT,
I AM GOING TO MISS HER
DEARLY,
ANYWAY!

I KNOW WE'LL CALL
AND WRITE
AND THOSE MOMENTS

WILL BE WARM
AND BEAUTIFUL;
BUT,
THERE'S SOMETHING
ABOUT WATCHING
ALL THOSE ADORABLE
EXPRESSIONS
ON HER FACE,
THE TWINKLING
IN HER EYES,
GETTING THOSE LOVING
HUGS
AND KISSES
AS SHE RUSHES
PAST ME
FROM URGENT MOMENT
TO URGENT MOMENT
THROUGH IMPATIENT
AND SOMETIMES EVEN
IMPETUOUS YOUTH...

I'M GOING TO MISS
ALL THAT...
I MISS IT
ALREADY!

I KNOW!
I KNOW!
I'LL ADJUST...
AND, IN THE NOT TOO DISTANT
FUTURE –
WHICH NOW SEEMS
LIKE AN ETERNITY
TO PASS –
I'LL WRITE ABOUT
THIS BEAUTIFUL PERSON,
THIS LOVELY WOMAN,
THIS CAREERIST,
THIS WIFE,
THIS MOTHER,
THIS FRIEND
WHOM I LOVE
SO VERY MUCH.

BUT,
I PROMISE YOU
THIS:

NO MATTER
WHAT SHE,
OR ANYONE
EVER SAYS,
I WILL
ALWAYS
GREET HER WITH,
"HI, BABY"

AND THAT
IS THAT!

MY FABULOUS PRE-VIEWER

I JUST LOVE EVERYTHING ABOUT HER!

I LOVE THE WAY SHE STARTS MY DAY...
HER SUNSHINY SMILE...
HER SPARKLING EYES...
THE EBULLIENCE OF HER PERSONALITY...
THE WONDERFUL WAY WE WORK TOGETHER...
HER INTELLIGENCE...
HER INSIGHTFULNESS...
THE CLARITY OF HER THOUGHTS...
THE SOUND OF HER VOICE.

I FEEL EXTRAORDINARILY FORTUNATE,
EXTREMELY GRATEFUL
AND ULTIMATELY BLESSED
THAT SHE WALKED INTO MY LIFE.

I DON'T EVER WANT TO SEE HER
WALK OUT OF IT!

THE FIRST TIME YOU SAID "HI DAD"

(A SONG FOR OUR DANCE ON
YOUR WEDDING DAY
(LINK TO YOUBE https://www.youtube.
com/watch?v=rUnuVeiXXIo)

I WAS NEVER SO HAPPY AS THE DAY YOU WERE BORN
'CAUSE I KNEW RIGHT THEN AND THERE...
IT WAS YOU WHO WOULD BRING GREAT JOY TO MY LIFE
AND BRIGHTEN EACH DAY OF EACH YEAR!

LIKE THE FIRST TIME YOU WALKED...AND TALKED...AND LAUGHED;
AND EVEN THE FIRST TIME YOU GOT MAD;
AND THE FIRST TIME YOU STOOD ON MY FEET TO DANCE;
AND THE FIRST TIME YOU SAID... "HI, DAD!"

I WAS NEVER SO PROUD AS I AM TODAY
OF THE WOMAN YOU HAVE BECOME...
OF ALL YOU'VE ACHIEVED...ALL ON YOUR OWN...
AND THE LOVE THAT YOU GIVE TO EVERYONE!

TODAY I WALKED YOU DOWN THE AISLE;
IT MUST HAVE BEEN MY LONGEST MILE...
BUT YOU'LL STILL BE MY "BABY";
I'LL ALWAYS CALL YOU "BABY"!

TODAY YOU BECAME A FINE MAN'S WIFE
WHEN BOTH OF YOU SAID, "I DO!"...
NOW THE WONDERFUL MEM'RIES YOU'VE GIVEN TO ME...
I'M WISHING TODAY FOR BOTH OF YOU...

LIKE THE FIRST TIME YOU WALKED...AND TALKED...AND LAUGHED;
AND EVEN THE FIRST TIME YOU GOT MAD;
AND THE FIRST TIME YOU STOOD ON MY FEET TO DANCE;
AND THE FIRST TIME YOU SAID... "HI, DAD!"

YOU'LL ALWAYS BE MY LITTLE GIRL,
THE SWEETEST THING IN THIS WHOLE WIDE WORLD;
AND EVEN THOUGH YOU'RE ALL GROWN UP...
A WOMAN AND A LADY -
YOU'LL ALWAYS BE ...MY "BABY"!

FOR MICHELLE...FEBRUARY, 1996

CHRISTMAS IS MY FAVORITE TIME OF YEAR

(A SONG FROM THE ALBUM, "MERRY CHRISTMAS FROM GRANDMA MIKIE)

(LINK TO YOUTUBE https://www.youtube.com/watch?v=hPhtc3jX9lg&ytbChannel=Grandma%20Mikie)

I'VE COUNTED DAYS 'TIL CHRISTMAS TIME
AND NOW IT'S FINALLY HERE…
FILLING HEARTS WITH LOTS OF LOVE
THAT WILL LAST THROUGHOUT THE YEAR!

I ALWAYS KNOW ITS CHRISTMAS TIME
WHEN TREES LIGHT UP THE NIGHT…
WITH PRETTY THINGS THAT SHINE AND GLOW
WITH COLORS REALLY BRIGHT!

OH, HOW I LOVE CHRISTMAS!
CHRISTMAS IS MY FAVORITE TIME OF YEAR…
WHEN CHRISTMAS SONGS ARE BEING SUNG…
STOCKINGS ARE HUNG…ONE BY ONE…
AND CHILDREN'S LAUGHTER FILLS THE AIR!

WHEN HAPPINESS IS EVERYWHERE
WHEN SANTA'S SOON IN SIGHT…
WHEN PEOPLE SMILE…AND WISH YOU WELL
AND YOU KNOW EVERYTHING'S ALRIGHT!

WHEN SANTA VISITS AFTER DARK
AND REINDEER PULL HIS SLEIGH...
FILLED WITH GIFTS FOR EVERYONE
THEN HE QUICKLY FLIES AWAY!

UNTIL NEXT YEAR...
WHEN I'LL BE WAITING...
UNTIL NEXT YEAR...
ANTICIPATING...

CHRISTMAS LULLABY

(A SONG)

GO TO SLEEP SWEET BABY;
IT'S CHRISTMAS EVE TONIGHT;
SANTA AND HIS REINDEER
WILL BE HERE BY MORNING LIGHT.

GO TO SLEEP SWEET BABY;
SLEEP ALL THROUGH THE NIGHT;
SANTA'S GIFTS WILL BRING YOU JOY...
ALL WRAPPED IN COLORS BRIGHT.

SO, SLEEP LITTLE BABY,
SLEEP TONIGHT...
SWEET DREAMS AND SLEEPY TIGHT;
KNOW YOU'RE LOVED
WITH EVERY HUG...
AND KISSED BY STARS ALL NIGHT.

GO TO SLEEP SWEET BABY;
AS MOONBEAMS BRUSH YOUR HAIR;
AND WHEN YOU WAKE TO WARM SUNLIGHT,
YOU'LL FEEL THE CHRISTMAS CHEER.

SO, SLEEP LITTLE BABY,
SLEEP TONIGHT...
SWEET DREAMS AND SLEEPY TIGHT;
KNOW YOU'RE LOVED
WITH EVERY HUG...
AND KISSED BY STARS ALL NIGHT.

CHRISTMAS TIME IS CHILDREN'S TIME

(A SONG)

CHRISTMAS TIME IS CHILDREN'S TIME...
IT'S THE HAPPIEST TIME OF YEAR...
THE TIME WHEN EVERYONE SHOWS THEIR LOVE...
AND JOY IS EVERYWHERE!

YES, CHRISTMAS TIME IS CHILDREN'S TIME...
IT'S A TIME TO SHOW WE CARE...
WITH PRESENTS WRAPPED IN COLORS BRIGHT...
FOR THOSE WE HOLD SO DEAR!

OH, CHRISTMAS TIME IS CHILDREN'S TIME...
IT'S THE BEST TIME OF YEAR...
A TIME TO SMILE, TO LAUGH AND LOVE...
A TIME WE ALL CAN SHARE!

YES, CHRISTMAS TIME IS CHILDREN'S TIME...
WHEN SANTA COMES TO TOWN...
WITH ALL HIS TOYS FOR GIRLS AND BOYS...
AND CHEER TO SPREAD AROUND!

OH, CHRISTMAS TIME IS CHILDREN'S TIME...
IT'S THE BEST TIME OF YEAR...
A TIME TO SMILE, TO LAUGH AND LOVE...
A TIME WE ALL CAN SHARE!

OH, CHRISTMAS TIME IS CHILDREN'S TIME...
IT'S THE BEST TIME OF YEAR...
A TIME TO SMILE, TO LAUGH AND LOVE...
A TIME WE ALL CAN SHARE!

THE ALPHABET SONG

"A" IS THE VERY FIRST LETTER OF THE ALPHABET;
"B" IS THE NEXT IN LINE;
THEN COMES "C" AND "D" AND "E"
AND "F" ... HOW VERY FINE!

"G" IS THE VERY NEXT LETTER OF THE ALPHABET;
"H" IS THE NEXT IN LINE;
THEN COMES "I" AND "J" AND "K"
AND "L"...HOW VERY FINE!

OH, IT'S FUN TO LEARN THE ALPHABET...
'CAUSE WHEN WE FINALLY DO...
WE'LL BE ABLE TO WRITE DOWN NAMES AND WORDS...
LIKE "I AM ME" AND "YOU ARE YOU!"

"M" IS THE VERY NEXT LETTER OF THE ALPHABET;
"N" IS THE NEXT IN LINE;
THEN COMES "O" AND "P" AND "Q"
AND "R"...HOW VERY FINE!

"S" IS THE VERY NEXT LETTER OF THE ALPHABET;
"T" IS THE NEXT IN LINE;
THEN COMES "U" AND "V" AND "W"
AND "X"...HOW VERY FINE!

NOW "Y" IS THE VERY NEXT LETTER OF THE ALPHABET;
AND "Z" IS THE LAST IN LINE;
AND NOW WE HAVE LEARNED
ALL THE LETTERS OF THE ALPHABET ---
(AND) "WOW! HOW VERY FINE!"

IT WAS FUN TO LEARN THE ALPHABET
'CAUSE NOW WHAT WE CAN DO...
IS BE ABLE TO WRITE DOWN NAMES AND WORDS...
LIKE "I AM ME" AND "YOU ARE YOU!"

"WHAT DID YOU SAY?"

(A SONG)

HOW WOULD YOU LIKE TO PLAY A GAME?
A GAME OF WORDS WITH A SILLY NAME.
IT'S REALLY FUN 'CAUSE WHAT YOU DO
IS MAKE MISTAKES THE WHOLE GAME THROUGH.

THE GAME OF THE NAME IS "WHAT DID YOU SAY?"
AND I THINK WE'VE ALREADY STARTED TO PLAY.
SO LET'S PUT OUR HEADS TOGETHER
AND SEE WHAT WE CAN DO –
WE'LL SWITCH THE LETTERS OF SOME WORDS...
AND YOU'LL FOOL ME WHILE I FOOL YOU.
    (WHAT DID YOU SAY?... WHAT DID YOU SAY?)

I COVE LANDY, I TOVE LEA...
I YOVE LOU AND LOU YOVE ME!
    (WHAT DID YOU SAY?... WHAT DID YOU SAY?)
I LOVE CANDY, I LOVE TEA...
I LOVE YOU AND YOU LOVE ME!
    (WHAT DID YOU SAY?... WHAT DID YOU SAY?)

IT'S SO EASY...AS COO SAN YEE...
I YOOLED FOU, NOW FOU YOOL ME.
    (WHAT DID YOU SAY?... WHAT DID YOU SAY?)
IT'S SO EASY...AS YOU CAN SEE...
I FOOLED YOU, NOW YOU FOOL ME!
    (WHAT DID YOU SAY?... WHAT DID YOU SAY?)
    (WHAT DID YOU SAY?... WHAT DID YOU SAY?)
I LOVE CANDY, I LOVE TEA...
I LOVE YOU AND YOU LOVE ME!
    (WHAT DID YOU SAY?... WHAT DID YOU SAY?)

IT'S SO EASY...AS COO SAN YEE...
I YOOLED FOU, NOW FOU YOOL ME.
    (WHAT DID YOU SAY?... WHAT DID YOU SAY?)
IT'S SO EASY...AS YOU CAN SEE...
I FOOLED YOU, NOW YOU FOOL ME!
    (WHAT DID YOU SAY?... WHAT DID YOU SAY?

POEMS OF LOVE, LIFE & RELATIONSHIPS

POEMS VI

INTROSPECTING

SEE AND BE

FOREGONE CONCLUSIONS
IN PROTECTIVE
ILLUSIONS
WILL LIMIT
THE VIEW
OF WHAT'S REALLY
TRUE;

BUT THE FEW
WHO BELIEVE
IN WHAT THEY
CONCEIVE

CAN BE
WHATEVER

THEY SEE!

ALL OR NOTHING

ALL OR NOTHING
SEEMS LIKE TOO MUCH
TO ASK
OF ONESELF,
LET ALONE
OF SOMEONE ELSE...
ESPECIALLY
SINCE NEITHER ONE
EXISTS.

TO ASK FOR
ALL OR NOTHING
MERELY
KEEPS ME OUT
COMPLETELY
AND
KEEPS YOU
LOCKED
WITHIN!

ALMOSTS

I OFTEN ASK
MYSELF

WHY
    I WASTE
        MY TIME

WITH ALMOSTS!

IS IT BECAUSE

    I KNOW

THAT THAT

IS REALLY

    ALL

        THERE IS?

AMERICA'S BEST...

(A SONG)

AT FIRST IT WAS SOMETHING
TO DREAM ABOUT;
NOW IT'S BECOME VERY REAL!
I'M SAYING GOODBYE
TO THE FEAR AND THE DOUBT;
IT'S THE PASSION TO WIN THAT I FEEL!

I'M GOING TO SET OUT NOW
AND FOLLOW MY QUEST;
I'M GOING TO SET MYSELF FREE!
I WILL LEARN WHAT I NEED
TO SURMOUNT EVERY TEST...
AND BE EVERY THING I CAN BE!

I'M GOING TO BE STRONG,
BE PROUD, BE JUST ME;
NO MORE COULD BE'S,
WOULD BE'S...
NO MAYBE'S;
NO ONE WILL MAKE ME
GET DOWN ON MY KNEES;
I'M GOING TO REACH SO HIGH
THAT I'M GOING TO BE...
AMERICA'S BEST!

AND WHENEVER A DREAM THAT I DREAM
COMES TRUE...
I'M GOING TO HAVE ANOTHER DREAM!
AND I WILL FOLLOW THAT DREAM
WITH A PASSION BRAND NEW...
'CAUSE DREAMS ARE THE AIR THAT I BREATHE!

EACH OF US

I REMEMBER STUDYING
ONE NIGHT,
THE MULTI-SHAPED,
MULTI-COLORED
TILE MONTAGE
ON THE WALL
ACROSS THE BAR –
SQUARES,
DIAMONDS,
HEXAGONS –
A COLLECTION
OF MANY FACES
BLENDING INTO ONE
COMPLETE PORTRAIT,
LIKE THE QUATRAINS
OF OMAR'S RUBAIYAT –
EACH SECTION
A COMPLETE STATEMENT,
EACH STATEMENT
AN INTEGRAL PART
OF THE OVERALL REALITY –
INDEPENDENTLY
NEEDING EACH OTHER
FOR FULFILLMENT.

AND SUCH,
IT SEEMS,
IS THE RELATIONSHIP
BETWEEN LIFE
AND THE PEOPLE
WHO LIVE IT -
NO ONE PERSON
FILLS ALL THE NEEDS
OF ANOTHER;

EACH OF US IS NO LESS
THAN A COMPLETE THOUGHT
IN THE PROCESS OF LIVING...
BUT NO MORE;
EACH OF US
REQUIRES ANOTHER...
AND MORE...
TO SIMPLY FILL A PAGE
OF THIS NEVER-ENDING
BOOK OF LIFE...
JUST THINK
OF HOW MANY OTHERS
WE MUST NEED
TO FORM
EVEN THE SMALLEST
CHAPTER.

WHY, THEN
DO WE RESIST
EACH OTHER,
CLOSING OURSELVES IN
OR OUT,
KEEPING EACH OTHER
AT A DISTANCE,
HOLDING EACH OTHER
APART?

WHY CAN WE NOT
LOVE EACH OTHER
FOR EVEN THE MOST
MINISCULE
CONTRIBUTION
WE MIGHT MAKE
TO EACH OTHER'S LIVES?

WHY MUST WE CREATE
AN ALL
OR NOTHING AT ALL
POSTURE?

AFTER ALL,
PERFECTION,
LIKE ONE HUNDRED PERCENT,
LIKE ZERO,
LIKE INFINITY,

IS NOTHING MORE
THAN A MERE
CONCEPT
WITHIN THE LIMITS
OF OUR CONDITIONED
EDUCATION –
IT MAY NOT EVEN
EXIST,
EXCEPT TO CREATE
A FICTIONAL PATH
TO THE ILLUSION
OF AN INTELLECTUAL
AND EMOTIONAL
HORIZON.

CAN WE NOT
CHANGE IT?

OR,

EVEN BETTER,

CAN WE NOT
ACCEPT SOMETHING LESS –
LIKE…SOMETHING…

TO ULTIMATELY HAVE
SO MUCH MORE?

I SEE YOU DEATH

I SEE YOU,
DEATH!
I SEE YOU CLEAR
IN THE SHADOWS
JUST AHEAD;
I KNOW YOU'VE COME
TO TAKE ME
WHERE NOTHINGNESS
IS ALL
INSTEAD!

BUT, CAN'T YOU SEE,
YOU'VE COME TOO SOON...
TOO MUCH
IS STILL UNDONE!
ALL MY LOVE
I'VE YET TO GIVE...
ON THE SAND
IT WAITS...
IN THE BRIGHT, WARM SUN.

THE LOVE
I SEEK,
MY CUP TO FILL,
STILL LIES BEYOND
MY ARM'S SHORT REACH!

I NEED MORE TIME –
YOU MUST STAND
STILL!
OH, WAVE OF LOVE,
ASCEND THE BEACH!

OH, DEATH,
JUST WAIT
FOR ONE MORE DAY –
DEAR LOVE
TO COME...
THEN I'LL
AWAY.

IN ABSOLUTE DEVOTION

IN ABSOLUTE DEVOTION

    TO MY DREAM,

I FIND

    I MUST ADMIT,

WITHOUT MUCH SENSE

    OR WIT,

THAT MY ABSOLUTE DEVOTION

    IS NOT

        A MERE EMOTION,

BUT OBSESSION

    MORE (UN)REAL

THAN IT SHOULD SEEM.

IT'S TIME

IT'S TIME WE FOLLOWED
    THE WAYS OF OUR FOUNDING FATHERS;

IT'S TIME WE RETURNED TO COMPROMISE;
IT'S TIME WE TALKED TO EACH OTHER
IT'S TIME WE ARGUED WITH EACH OTHER
    IN A CIVIL MANNER;
IT'S TIME WE LEARNED TO UNDERSTAND EACH OTHER
    AND ACCEPTED EACH OTHER'S NEEDS, WANTS,
        DESIRES AND BELIEFS;

IT'S TIME WE ACCEPTED THE FACT
    THAT TO COMPROMISE
        IS TO MAKE A DEAL;

AND IT'S TIME THAT WE UNDERSTOOD
    AND ACCEPTED THE FACT
        THAT THE BEST SIGN OF A GOOD DEAL
        IS WHEN EVERYONE WALKS AWAY
           A LITTLE UNHAPPY.

LIFE WON'T STAND STILL

FOR QUITE SOMETIME
THAT FOLLOWED,
I WOULD LOOK BACK
WITH TEARS
AT THE MOMENT
WHEN MY HEART FELL SUDDEN
AND MY HOPES
HAD TURNED TO FEARS;

BUT THEN,
A FORCE
INSIDE ME
BEGAN TO WORK
AT FEVERED PACE...
RESULTING
IN MY STRENGTH
RETURNING FAST...
IN MY
BREATHING OUT
THE PAST,

SOME
WILL SAY,
"THE WORK
OF GOD",

OTHERS WILL,
"HIS WILL";
PERHAPS,
THEY'RE RIGHT;
PERHAPS
THEY'RE NOT;

PERHAPS,
LIFE
SIMPLY WON'T
STAND STILL.

LOVE IS LIKE A CHILD

LOVE IS NEVER TAKEN –
NEVER TAKEN AWAY OR BACK;
IT IS LIKE A CHILD
WHICH YOU CREATED,
NURTURED
AND HELPED DEVELOP
TO THE POINT
OF HAVING A LIFE
AND EXISTENCE OF ITS OWN,
GOING OUT TO THE WORLD...
AS YOUR GIFT –
A PART OF YOU...
BUT NO LONGER YOURS ALONE...
AND PROBABLY
NEVER REALLY WAS;
IT IS NOT A POSSESSION
THAT YOU CAN OWN
AND THEREFORE,
IT IS NEVER LOST.

TO KNOW IT'S BEAUTY AND JOY
YOU MUST ACCEPT
IT'S INDEPENDENCE OF YOU
AND RELATE TO IT
WITH NO ATTEMPT

TO CONTROL ITS ACTIONS
OR CHANGE ITS DESTINY;
BUT RATHER,
TO BE THERE
TO ENCOURAGE,
TO SUPPORT
AND CONTINUE TO HELP IT GROW.

YOU NEVER GIVE LOVE...
YOU ONLY GIVE IT LIFE;
AND YOU COULD NOT ASK
OR BE ASKED
TO GIVE A GREATER GIFT
TO ANYONE.

LOVE POEMS

SOMETIMES

I THINK

I WRITE

A LOT

OF THIS

STUFF

JUST

TO PUNISH

MYSELF

FOR NOT

REALLY

CHANGING.

LOVE

LOVE

IS A COLLECTION

OF THOSE MOMENTS

OF BEAUTY

WHICH SURVIVE

OUR FOOLISH DREAMS!

NO CONTEST

CRYING IS OK....

ONCE IN A WHILE –

BUT,

NOT MUCH FUN!

DEPRESSION

IS DEFINITELY

A BUMMER!

KISS ME!

I'D RATHER

SMILE!

OPPORTUNITY

NEVER

IS AN OPPORTUNITY

LOST...

IT WILL BE

FOUND

BY SOMEONE...

EVEN

IF IT ISN'T

YOU!

PASSING FORTY

THE NEED TO
CAPTURE
LOST YOUTH
HAS NOT CAPTURED
ME...
AT LEAST, NOT YET...
AND I HOPE
IT NEVER WILL.

AFTER ALL,
WITHOUT A PAST
DIFFERENT FROM TODAY
WE WOULD HAVE
NO PERSPECTIVE
TO DETERMINE
WHAT WE HAVE
ACHIEVED,
ACCOMPLISHED,
DEVELOPED OR BUILT;
EVEN WORSE,
WE'D NEVER
KNOW
WHETHER WE EVER
LOVED
OR WERE LOVED...
AND WHAT A TERRIBLE
TRAGEDY
THAT WOULD BE!

AND WITHOUT SUCH
VISIONS
AND KNOWLEDGE,
THE FUTURE WOULD BE
NOTHING MORE
THAN JUST ANOTHER DAY
ABOUT TO HAPPEN –
WITHOUT HOPE,
WITHOUT EXCITEMENT,
WITHOUT SIGNIFICANCE...
AND WHAT A TRAGEDY
THAT WOULD BE!

THERE IS THE POSSIBILITY,
OF COURSE,
THAT I NEVER DID
PASS FORTY...
MAYBE,
I WAS JUST
TOO BUSY...
OR, PERHAPS,
INSTEAD,
IT JUST PASSED
ME;
EITHER THAT,
OR IT WON'T EVEN
ARRIVE
UNTIL FIFTY...
IF EVER;

NO MATTER...
IN BETWEEN,
THERE ARE
GREAT YEARS
TO LIVE.

AND LIVE THEM
I WILL...

TO THE FULLEST!

RUNNIN'

(A SONG)

THE ROAD IS NOT THE SAME
WHEN YOU TRY TO TRAVEL BACK;
WHAT WAS RIGHT YESTERDAY
IS NOW A DIFFERENT TRACK;
WHAT USED TO BE THE FIRST IN LINE
    NOW SEEMS TO BE THE LAST;
WHAT WAS ONCE THE FUTURE
    HAS NOW BECOME THE PAST!

I'M RUNNIN' HARD, I'M RUNNIN' FAST...
BUT AM I RUNNIN' TO THE FUTURE...
    OR RUNNIN' FROM THE PAST?

YOU NEVER CAN RETURN
TO THE LIFE THAT USED TO BE;
WHAT WE WERE YESTERDAY
IS NO LONGER YOU OR ME.

BUT NO MATTER HOW MUCH WE CHANGE,
    WE SEEM TO STAY THE SAME...
LIKE WE CAME 'ROUND THE BOARD,
    AND OUR LIFE WAS JUST A GAME!

AND NOW THE PAST LIES AHEAD...
TO LURE US FOOLS
WHERE THE WISE WON'T TREAD;

AND NOW I CAN'T BE SURE
OF THE ROAD I'M TRAVELIN' IN...
    AM I LOOKIN' WHERE I'M GOIN'...
    OR JUST SEEIN' WHERE I'VE BEEN?

THE KEY

WHEN INTO THE LOCK

FITS YOUR KEY,

OPEN THE DOOR

AND WALK IN!

THE PREDATOR

OF THE PREDATOR
    BEWARE;

ENTER NOT HER ALLURING
    LAIR...

I IMPLORE YOU!

RESIST YOU CAN'T
    HER EVERY CHARM;

HER BEAUTY FEAR
    WITH GREAT ALARM...

I FOREWARN YOU!

EUPHORIC WILL YOUR
    YOUR FINAL HOUR BE

AS SENSUOUSLY
    SHE DEVOURS THEE!

I ASSURE YOU!

BUT, IF BY CHANCE
    OR ACT OF FATE,

YOU SHOULD SURVIVE,
    ALLOW ME STATE:

I ENVY YOU!

THE TRUTH

YOU SHOULD NOT FEEL HURT

BY THE FACT

THAT SOMEONE

LOVES YOU ENOUGH

TO ACCEPT,

WITH APPARENT EASE,

YOUR URGENT NEED

TO SAY GOODBYE

TWO ALTERNATIVES

THERE ARE BUT
TWO ALTERNATIVES:

THE FIRST IS
LOVE...

THE SECOND...
NOTHING!

UNREQUITED LOVE

UNREQUITED LOVE

IS A MISNOMER!

LOVE,

BY IT'S VERY NATURE...

DENIES

AND PRECLUDES

ANY

QUID-PRO-QUO!

WAR

WAR

IS THE MIRROR
OF MAN'S MIND,

REFLECTING
HIS INABILITY
TO KEEP PEACE
WITH HIMSELF;

HE IS APPALLED
BY HIS OWN
UGLINESS,

DISTRAUGHT
BY HIS OWN WEAKNESS,

ENDANGERED
BY HIS OWN
RECKLESSNESS,

INCENSED
BY HIS OWN
SELF-HATRED...

WAR
IS MAN'S
SELF-PUNISHMENT...

SUICIDE
BY EXECUTION!

YOU CAN'T GIVE LOVE TO ANYONE

YOU CAN'T GIVE LOVE TO ANYONE...

'CAUSE YOU CAN'T EVER TAKE IT BACK...

IT'S NOT A THING

LIKE WASHED-OUT JEANS

YOU CAN BUY RIGHT OFF A RACK;

LOVE IS INDEPENDENT -

GOT A LIFE ALL ITS OWN –

GOES WHERE IT FEELS WELCOME...

LEAVES THE REST ALONE.

LOVE IS WHAT YOU'RE FEELING

WHEN YOU'RE FEELING BEST OF ALL;

AND BEST OF ALL...

YOU FEEL IT MOST

WHEN YOU NEED IT MOST OF ALL.

YOUR CHOICE

LOVE

IS AN ENTITY OF ITS OWN,

INDEPENDENT OF YOU,

SEPARATE FROM YOU;

IT IS A GIFT OF BEAUTY

GIVEN BY YOUR LOVER

AND BY YOU.

YOU HAVE THE CHOICE

OF TAKING IT WITH YOU

AND KEEPING IT

FOREVER

OR LETTING IT GO

AND LOSING IT

IN A MISCONCEPTION

OF SOMEONE ELSE'S NEED

TO SAY GOODBYE.

ABOUT THE AUTHOR

Richard Bayer is CEO of MIRICOMPANIES, LLC and subsidiaries, which are engaged in music and television production, and music publishing. He is a semi-retired Certified Public Accountant engaged in tax consulting in the New York City Metropolitan area. He has a BBA degree from the Bernard M. Baruch School of Business and Public Administration of The City University of New York.

Mr. Bayer is also CEO of GRANDMA MIKIE'S MAGIC MUSIC BOX, LLC which he formed with his wife and partner, Mikie Harris, a noted professional songwriter, singer and record producer. The company creates music and educational and entertaining videos for children and their families on YouTube.

In addition to having founded his own CPA firm, Mr. Bayer has lectured on various aspects of taxation and accounting to groups of accountants for the New York State Society of

Certified Public Accountants and to students and faculty at Columbia University Graduate School of Business and the State University of New York (SUNY) in Albany.

He has also conducted seminars for various groups in the entertainment industry regarding taxation, business management and financial planning.

Mr. Bayer and his wife live in New Jersey and have four adult children and a little Maltese dog named "Sisi" who appears in all their videos, as well as a grandson and two granddogs, named Petey and Wrinkles...all three being rescue dogs.